George Washington Carver

Peanut Scientist

Natalya Jones

REAL LIFE readers™

Rosen Classroom™

New York

Published in 2009 by The Rosen Publishing Group, Inc.
29 East 21st Street, New York, NY 10010

Book Design: Michael J. Flynn

Photo Credits: Cover © Stock Montage/Contributor/Hulton Archive/Getty Images; p. 5 © Bettmann/Corbis; pp. 6, 10 © MPI/Stringer/Hulton Archive/Getty Images; p. 8 © Joe Gough/Shutterstock; p. 9 © Sue Ashe/Shutterstock; p. 13 (Carver) © Hulton Archive/Getty Images; p. 13 (stamp) © LH/Shutterstock.

ISBN: 978-1-4358-0085-4
6-pack ISBN: 978-1-4358-0086-1

Manufactured in the United States of America

Contents

The Birth of a Famous Scientist

George Washington Carver was a famous **scientist** who studied plants. He listed over 300 uses for peanuts! George taught farmers a way to farm that kept the soil **fertile**. This helped farmers grow more crops.

Carver was born as a **slave** on Moses Carver's farm around 1864. His father died soon after he was born. Baby George and his mother were **kidnapped**. Moses Carver found George but couldn't find his mother. Moses and his wife raised George.

George, shown here as an adult, was taught to read and write by Moses Carver and his wife, Susan.

From Student to Teacher

As a young boy, George loved to study plants. Neighbors called him the "plant doctor." When he was about 12, George went to a school for black children. He worked several jobs and saved his money.

In 1890, Carver became the first black student at Simpson **College**. In 1891, he changed colleges in order to study plants. He became the first black teacher at the new college. In 1896, Carver went to teach at a black college in Tuskegee, Alabama.

Carver taught at this school in Alabama for almost 50 years.

Success in Alabama

The college gave Carver some land to use for teaching. Cotton plants had taken most of the **nutrients** out of the soil, and not much would grow in it. Carver planted pea plants because he knew the roots would put nutrients back into the soil. Then he could grow cotton again.

Carver told farmers that peanuts would also make their soil fertile. His idea worked, but soon farmers had too many peanuts to sell!

peanut field

Many farmers in the South made money by growing cotton. Carver's way of farming helped them keep growing large cotton crops.

Carver even found a way to make building blocks out of old cotton stems!

Peanut Butter!

Carver did **experiments** to find ways to use the extra peanuts. He listed more than 300 uses. They included cooking oil, soap, shampoo, ink, glue, and gas. Carver also made a food that we still eat today—peanut butter!

Carver discovered that growing sweet potatoes, **soybeans**, and **pecans** also made soil rich. He used sweet potatoes to make more than 100 things. He used soybeans to make paints. He found about seventy-five uses for pecans, too.

Carver said growing peanuts would make the soil rich.

↓

Farmers grew lots of peanuts and made the soil fertile.

↓

Farmers had too many peanuts to sell.

↓

Carver experimented with the extra peanuts.

↓

Carver listed more than 300 uses for peanuts.

Honoring George Washington Carver

On weekends, Carver took a cart to different farmers and showed them his ideas. He called the cart "School on Wheels." In 1940, he gave all the money he had saved to his college in Tuskegee so his work could continue after he died.

Carver died in 1943. His birthplace was made a national monument. It was the first national monument for an African American. Today, George Washington Carver is remembered as a great scientist and a great man.

George Washington Carver's picture was put on U.S. stamps in 1948 and 1998.

DR. GEORGE WASHINGTON CARVER
UNITED STATES POSTAGE
3¢

The Life of George Washington Carver

1864 — George Washington Carver is born. He and his mother are kidnapped, but Moses Carver gets him back.

1875 — Carver leaves home and goes to a school for black children.

1890 — Carver becomes the first black student at Simpson College.

1891 — Carver changes colleges in order to study plants.

1894 — Carver becomes the first black teacher at the college where he studied plants.

1896 — Carver becomes a teacher at a black college in Tuskegee, Alabama.

1921 — Carver begins teaching others about the uses of peanuts.

1940 — Carver gives all the money he has saved to his school in Tuskegee.

1943 — Carver dies.

1953 — Carver's birthplace is made a national monument.

Glossary

college (KAH-lihj) A school you can go to after high school.

experiment (ihk-SPEHR-uh-muhnt) A test done by scientists to find out about something.

fertile (FUHR-tuhl) Good for growing things.

kidnap (KIHD-nap) To take someone away by force.

nutrient (NOO-tree-uhnt) Something a living thing needs to live and grow.

pecan (pih-KAHN) A kind of nut that grows on trees in the southern United States.

scientist (SY-uhn-tihst) A person who studies the way things are and the way things act.

slave (SLAYV) Someone who is "owned" by another person.

soybean (SOY-bean) A kind of bean.

Index

Due to the changing nature of Internet links, The Rosen Publishing Group, Inc., has developed an online list of Web sites related to the subject of this book. This site is updated regularly. Please use this link to access the list: **http://www.rcbmlinks.com/rlr/pnut**